DEVELOPING DIGITAL AND MEDIA LITERACY SKILLS

Spotting Online Scams and Fraud

Stuart A. Kallen

San Diego, CA

For more information, contact:
ReferencePoint Press, Inc.
PO Box 27779
San Diego, CA 92198
www.ReferencePointPress.com

LIBRARY OF CONGRESS CATALOGING-IN-PUBLICATION DATA

Names: Kallen, Stuart A., 1955- author.
Title: Spotting online scams and fraud / by Stuart A. Kallen.
Description: San Diego, CA : ReferencePoint Press, [2024] | Series: Developing digital and media literacy skills | Includes bibliographical references and index.
Identifiers: LCCN 2023004101 (print) | LCCN 2023004102 (ebook) | ISBN 9781678205409 (library binding) | ISBN 9781678205416 (ebook)
Subjects: LCSH: Internet fraud--Prevention--Juvenile literature. | Computer crimes--Prevention--Juvenile literature.
Classification: LCC HV6773.15.C56 K35 2024 (print) | LCC HV6773.15.C56 (ebook) | DDC 364.16/3--dc23/eng/20230320
LC record available at https://lccn.loc.gov/2023004101
LC ebook record available at https://lccn.loc.gov/2023004102

CONTENTS

Losing Billions to Scammers

Historians say scammers have been tricking people out of their money since the first gold coins were minted in Greece around twenty-five hundred years ago. These swindlers had to work hard to cheat ordinary people out of their hard-earned cash. Before the age of mass communication, scammers, referred to as grifters, confidence men, or con artists, had to befriend their targets, whom they referred to as marks. After stealing money from marks, con artists often had to leave town, change their names, and otherwise avoid their victims. These limitations restricted the number of scams that could be perpetrated on the public at any one time.

New Platforms, New Targets

In the twenty-first century, advanced technology provides scammers with online tools that grifters from an early era could never imagine. Scammers adopt fake identities and use them to defraud people using texts, emails, social media sites, e-commerce sites, dating apps, and banking apps. The internet has made it easy to run scams involving banking, real estate, the stock market, and even romance. Scammers can operate from almost anywhere in the world, and victims who are conned have little chance of getting their money back.

With billions of people living their lives online, scamming has grown into a worldwide industry. According to the Federal Trade Commission (FTC) more than 2.8 million consumers filed fraud reports in 2021. Americans lost over $5.8 billion to online scams, a 70 percent increase from the previous year.

"The generation we think of as being the most savvy with the internet . . . is where the numbers are growing the fastest when it comes to scams."[1]

—David McClellan, CEO of Social Catfish

Scammers target anyone and everyone. Although it is commonly believed that older people are the most common victims of online scams, this is not true. A 2021 study from the identity-verification service Social Catfish shows that young people are more likely to fall for online scams than their grandparents. The number of online scams perpetrated on victims aged twenty or younger increased by more than 150 percent between 2017 and 2020. This translates to a loss of $71 million compared to $8 million in 2017. By comparison, online scams against those sixty and over grew 112 percent during this period. David McClellan, chief executive officer (CEO) of Social Catfish, commented on the numbers: "It is alarming. The generation we think of as being the most savvy with the internet . . . is where the numbers are growing the fastest when it comes to scams. . . . This age group is very comfortable being online and being very public about their lives. So that makes them very trusting when they're on the Internet."[1]

Falling for a Convincing Story

Con artists have always taken advantage of peoples' trust, hope for the future, and generosity to trick them into handing over money. This type of psychological manipulation is called *social engineering* when it is done online. Cybercriminals can be good storytellers, and social engineering often involves convincing victims they can find love, get rich, get a great travel deal, or land their dream job. Scammers pretend to be likable, knowledgeable, caring, and helpful to win a victim's trust. They pose as authority figures working for government agencies, banks, tech companies, or law firms. Whatever the exact method, the scammer's goal is the same: to trick someone into giving away their passwords, answers to security questions, Social Security number, bank account and credit card numbers, and other personal information.

Scammers are most often found on social media sites such as Instagram, WhatsApp, and Google Hangouts. Facebook is the world's most popular social media app, which also makes it the number one platform for scammers. Criminals use the site to pose as friends or relatives seeking emergency loans. Fraudsters on Facebook ask people to pay fees to apply for jobs or to receive valuable gifts. Sometimes cybercrooks post links that install malware on a victim's computer. Facebook Marketplace is especially dangerous. Over 1 billion people use the platform to buy and sell goods every month. This means billions of dollars are changing hands on Marketplace. Scammers collect deposits on

The internet has made it easy for scammers to defraud victims, who usually have little chance of getting their money back.

phony apartment rentals, sell items that are broken, or get paid for products they do not possess. Some sell counterfeit goods marketed as expensive designer items. Others pose as influencers; they create fake accounts to mimic actual influencers to trick victims into giving up money and personal information.

Scams are so common that terms such as *social engineering, phishing, spoofing,* and *robocall* are part of the general lexicon. Yet despite the awareness of scammer techniques, cybercriminals continue to steal billions online. The Internet Crime Complaint Center of the Federal Bureau of Investigation (FBI) reports that victims lost $4.2 billion to online scammers in 2020. Experts say the number of actual rip-offs is undoubtedly higher, but many victims fail to report online crime because they are embarrassed that they were so easily fooled. There is hope, however. As psychologist Kenneth Freundlich writes, "Social engineering can be difficult to resist because it is based on our natural tendencies, such as curiosity, respect for authority, and desire to help our friends. By being aware of these powerful psychological principles at play, people can better protect themselves and avoid falling prey to scammers."[2]

Phishing, Spear Phishing, and Ransomware

In 2021 Lawrence Abrams received an important-looking email message from Norton Security. The company is well-known for its products that protect users from most types of malware—malicious software used to steal personal information or disrupt computer functions. Abrams's attention-getting email had a prominent Norton logo at the top of the message and appeared legitimate. The email said Abrams was being charged nearly $350 for a program called Norton LifeLock. Abrams knew he had not ordered the program, so he called the phone number included with the email.

Abrams talked to a man on the phone who said he worked for Norton tech support. Abrams said he never installed Norton LifeLock on his computer. The agent told Abrams he could stop the $350 charge by clicking on a link in the email. This took Abrams to what appeared to be a Best Buy Geek Squad website. Following the instructions of the tech support guy, Abrams downloaded and installed software programs from the website. Abrams was then told to input his name, address, phone number, and date of birth on a Notepad program. Abrams logged off.

Falling for Scams

Lawrence Abrams is the owner and editor in chief of the digital security website BleepingComputer.com. He knew immediately that the email purportedly from Norton was fake. Abrams deliberately followed the instructions on the email and talked to the phony tech support agent to learn the details of the scam. During the process, Abrams saw that the scammer had secretly installed a program called TeamViewer on his computer. This allowed the cybercrook to view Abrams's desktop screen while gaining access to all the information on the computer.

The personal information Abrams provided to the scammer was not accurate, and the phone and computer he used were test devices used specifically to investigate fraudsters. As an expert at malware removal, Abrams would not be fooled by bogus emails sent by scammers. But as he attests, "Unfortunately, many people fall for these scams and provide threat actors remote access to their computers. Sadly, it is even more common for older people to fall for this scam as they may not have much experience with computers."[3]

Abrams says hundreds of thousands of fake antivirus billing emails are sent out every day. They appear to be from Norton, Microsoft, McAfee, and the Geek Squad. The scammers who send them are engaged in a type of social engineering called phishing. The attackers send deceptive messages, such as the one received by Abrams, to install malware on a victim's computer. This allows them to obtain passwords, bank account numbers, and other sensitive information. Although some use the logos and names of popular security software companies, other phishing emails mimic popular companies, including Apple, Netflix, Chase Bank, Facebook, eBay, and Amazon.

> "Unfortunately, many people fall for [phishing] scams and provide threat actors remote access to their computers."[3]
>
> —Lawrence Abrams, editor in chief of BleepingComputer.com

According to the FBI, phishing emails are the favorite scam run by cybercriminals;

Norton software is available for purchase in stores or online. Every day, scammers send out hundreds of thousands of emails that appear to be from Norton or another software security company.

90 percent of cyberattacks involve phishing. The primary form of attack involves emails with fake invoices, and around 1.5 million new phishing websites are created every month. In 2021 the FBI received a record 324,000 complaints from phishing victims. And this statistic only represents Americans who filed a complaint with the agency. There were undoubtedly countless more who did not report the crime.

According to the email security company Valimail, 3.4 billion phishing emails of all sorts were sent out every day in 2021. A type of fraud called *smishing* involves malicious links in text messages. Smishing scams accounted for 376 million fraudulent texts sent to phones daily in 2021.

Spear Fishing

Fraudsters view phishing as a numbers game. A single scammer who sends out thousands of fake emails only needs to hook a few dozen victims to make the effort pay off. But some cybercriminals take a more personal approach by spear phishing. This type of social engineering targets a specific person, group, or business.

Spear phishers conduct what is called reconnaissance, or recon; they carefully research their targets on sites such as Facebook and LinkedIn, making note of their interests, online activities, and personal contacts. Some might also search for information on the dark web, a shadowy part of the internet where scammers can buy and sell illegally obtained personal data and credit card numbers.

Spear phishers with advanced skills take aim at large companies. They use artificial intelligence programs that can scan massive amounts of data. This allows them to identify the habits of CEOs and other high-level executives. The stolen information allows spear phishers to craft highly personalized emails or texts with details that make the messages seem legitimate. When prospective victims see messages that appear to come from friends, coworkers, or business associates, they let their guard down. This leads them to click on a malware link or download a dangerous attachment.

According to Norton Security, spear phishing scams target over four hundred businesses every day, including many top tech

Spoofing Victims

Cybercriminals have their own vocabulary to describe the online rip-offs they run. A scam called spoofing is generally carried out to steal money from a victim. Spoofing messages often appear to come from a bank or a major e-commerce site such as Amazon. Spoofers generally follow the same script. A person posing as a company representative claims to have seen suspicious activity on the user's account that needs to be urgently addressed. Victims are instructed to provide personal information or make a payment to solve the problem.

In another type of scam, a spoofer offers a victim a fake coupon for a highly desirable item like an iPhone or PlayStation. The spoofer requires the target to make a "discounted" payment before the item can be shipped. Some ambitious spoofers set up fake websites that closely resemble a user's legitimate bank. The sites tell victims to log in with their user names and passwords. These are promptly used by the spoofer to steal money from the victim's accounts.

companies. And social engineering allows scammers to penetrate even the most sophisticated security systems with little effort. In 2022 a New Jersey teenager used his recon to access internal communications at the ride-hailing company Uber. The scammer was able to access a secure cellphone that belonged to Uber's systems administrator. A systems administrator is an information technology (IT) professional who maintains computer networks and servers at a company. The eighteen-year-old hacker repeatedly texted the administrator's phone in the middle of the night, masquerading as an Uber IT worker. He said he needed what is called multifactor authentication (MFA), which grants access to a website through passwords, personal identification numbers, or other forms of verification. When malicious hackers continually bombard people with requests for information, it is called an MFA fatigue attack. Targets become so tired of receiving the request that they give in and provide the information.

In the Uber case, the hacker used the MFA fatigue attack to gain access to the company's entire computer network. The scammer wanted to brag about his accomplishment, so he emailed secret company documents to security engineer Sam Curry, who said the MFA fatigue attack provided the hacker with "the golden ticket jackpot. . . . There's nothing [he] can't access. It's Disneyland. It's a blank check at the candy shop and Christmas morning all rolled up together."[4]

Holding Companies Hostage

The Uber hacker was motivated by his personal beliefs. After revealing the hack, he demanded that Uber improve its security measures to protect customer data. The hacker also insisted that Uber provide higher wages for its drivers.

Uber was able to quickly recover from the attack, but sometimes scammers can bring a company's business to a halt. These cybercriminals use social engineering methods to install ransomware on a computer or network belonging to an individual or organization. Ransomware encrypts all the files on the target's computers; documents are scrambled and cannot be read by legitimate users of the devices. The scammer demands a ransom payment for the decryption key that will unscramble the files and allow the target to resume business. If the ransom is not paid, the scammer might destroy the company's data or release it to the public.

The ransomware attack on the Colonial Pipeline exemplifies the harm caused by cybercriminals. The Colonial Pipeline, which runs from Texas to New Jersey, is one of the largest and most important oil pipelines in the United States. The pipeline provides gasoline, diesel, jet fuel, and home heating oil to around half of all consumers on the East Coast. In 2021 a cybergang called DarkSide easily breached the security systems protecting the Colonial Pipeline computer network. Colonial did not use MFA—the entire system was protected by a single password that was leaked on the dark web.

DarkSide infected the company's IT network and digital pipeline systems with ransomware. The attackers also stole one hundred gigabytes of company data that they threatened to release. This would provide vital information that could be used by the

During a 2021 DarkSide attack of the Colonial Pipeline, a Florida gas station's signs read "out" because it has no fuel.

"Many of the companies running our critical infrastructure have left their systems vulnerable to hackers through dangerously negligent cybersecurity."[5]

—Ron Wyden, US senator from Oregon

company's competitors or other hackers. As a result of the attack, the pipeline was shut down. This caused fuel shortages that prompted President Joe Biden to declare a temporary state of emergency. Colonial paid a $5 million ransom in cryptocurrency, or crypto, to DarkSide. Operations resumed five days after the initial attack. (The FBI later recovered around half of the ransom by identifying one of the online accounts where the crypto was deposited.)

Ransomware threats have surged in number as malicious agents, or "threat actors," have targeted energy systems, tech companies, hospitals, schools, and government agencies. Oftentimes, the cheapest and easiest way for entities to resume business is to simply pay the ransom. After the Colonial Pipeline attack, the Senate Armed Services Subcommittee on Cybersecurity investigated the problem. Oregon senator Ron Wyden issued this statement after the hearings: "The shutdown of the Colonial Pipeline by cyber-criminals highlights a massive problem—many of the companies running our critical infrastructure have left their systems vulnerable to hackers through dangerously negligent cybersecurity."[5]

Like Any Other Business

In 2021 investigative reporter Michael Schwirtz was able to access a secret communications network used by the Russian-speaking threat actors who run DarkSide. He found that the cybergang operates like a legitimate online business in many ways. In addition to running its own scams, DarkSide makes its malware available to subscribers. Criminals sign up for the DarkSide subscription service that gives them access to malware used to carry out ransom attacks. Depending on the amount of the ransom obtained, DarkSide takes a 10 to 25 percent cut. Schwirtz explains, "DarkSide can work with dozens of affiliates who are working round the clock trying to find vulnerabilities in various companies and inserting the malware. And they just have to sit back and wait for these attacks to be successful."[6]

DarkSide has an online dashboard similar to those used by lawful companies. The dashboard has graphs and charts that list the latest scams and the money earned. DarkSide even runs a tech support site where hackers can chat online with customer service representatives. By accessing the dashboard, Schwirtz learned that DarkSide had received more than $90 million in crypto payments in 2021.

DarkSide also sends out press releases that advertise new products to its cybercriminal subscribers. In 2021 the company was offering malware used for a type of cyberattack called a DDos, or distributed denial of service. This malicious software overloads a computer system by flooding it with millions of service requests, causing a traffic jam to the site that prevents access by legitimate users. When scammers initiate a DDos incident, they demand a ransom to end the flood of requests.

Scams That Target Teens

The FBI reported that teenagers lost more than $101 million to online scams in 2021. And it should come as no surprise that the scammers target kids on popular social media platforms such as Facebook, TikTok, Snapchat, and Instagram. Teens who post photos and videos of their artwork, music, or live performances might attract attention from scammers who say they are recruiters for talent shows or art contests. The swindlers convince victims to pay an entry fee by promising a big prize or access to an important audition.

Some scammers search for teens who are heading off to college. They promise scholarships or grants but ask for money up front as a fee to process the application. Sometimes scammers ask victims to fill out long forms that contain sensitive data such as a Social Security number or bank account log-in information.

Teen job scams are also popular. Rip-off artists offer someone a great job, but they say the victim must first pay for certification, training materials, or other expenses. As with all other scams targeting teens, the scammers never deliver what was promised, and the victims lose their personal information and money.

DDos attacks are the favorite type of cybercrime used by a ransomware gang called Lapsus$. The cybergang, which is believed to have originated in Brazil, seems to have spread to London and beyond. Lapsus$ has breached the computer networks of major companies including Samsung, T-Mobile, Nvidia, Microsoft, and Rockstar Games.

Unlike DarkSide, Lapsus$ is a loosely organized group whose members are mainly young adults. According to Bloomberg News, the leader of Lapsus$ was a sixteen-year-old hacker going by the online name of "White." He took down some of the world's biggest companies from his mother's house in Oxford, England. When police arrested the teen, whose identity was withheld because of his age, it was discovered that he had amassed a $14 million fortune. Police arrested six others connected to Lapsus$ scams who were between sixteen and twenty-one years old. But the arrests did not stop the scammers; the Lapsus$ channel on the messaging app Telegram has more than forty-seven thousand subscribers. One of the subscribers is nine years old.

Long Prison Sentences

In recent years there has been a push by educators and politicians to protect kids from online threats. But some teens are turning to cybercrime. In 2021 a Canadian teenager was arrested for stealing $36 million in cryptocurrency. Another teen, named Ellis Pinsky, began scamming online at age fifteen and had accumulated over $100 million by the time he turned eighteen. Although these young adults might have enjoyed showing off their hacking skills while grabbing large sums of money, they wound up in police custody. The stolen money was returned to the victims.

Online scams that involve social engineering, phishing, spear phishing, spoofing, and other cybercrime might seem fun or rewarding, but there are risks and consequences. Cybercrime is a federal offense. A first-time offender convicted of running a DDos scam or a ransomware attack can receive a sentence of up to ten years in federal prison. The penalty for a second offense can be up to twenty years.

> "[Hackers are] evil computer geniuses with sociopath traits who heartlessly ruin their innocent victims' lives and gleefully boast of their multi-million dollar heists."[7]
>
> —Michael Terpin, scam victim

One of Pinsky's victims, Michael Terpin, called hackers "evil computer geniuses with sociopath traits who heartlessly ruin their innocent victims' lives and gleefully boast of their multi-million dollar heists."[7] As Terpin makes clear, online scammers damage the lives and livelihoods of their targets. But there is little chance of stopping them with millions of dollars to be made. Statistics show phishing campaigns accounted for losses of $17,700 per minute in 2021. Worldwide, ransomware attacks cost $22,184 per minute.

Thwart Phishing Scams

Jim Browning is one of those people who are plagued by a constant stream of messages from evil scammers trying to trick him out of his money. But Browning is not a typical consumer; he is a scam baiter, a digital detective who uses his advanced computers skills to interrupt cybercrooks while they are scamming victims. Browning posts scam baiter videos to YouTube. In one 2021 video, Browning can be heard calling a potential mark on the phone as a complex scam was taking place. In this particular con, the scammer falsely claimed to have taken control of the victim's bank account, which held over $17,000. The only way the victim could get his money back was to mail the scammer gift cards worth several thousand dollars. Browning explained to the victim that the scammer was showing him a fake webpage that showed his bank account zeroed out. Browning says he spends twelve hours a day disrupting scammers, and he has stopped at least one thousand scams. "I'll never know for sure exactly what the impact of what I'm doing is, but I think it's still worth doing," Browning explains. "Even if the police do nothing, which they mostly do, I'm doing something."[8]

This photo shows gift cards for sale in a Best Buy store. Scammers often try to persuade victims to purchase gift cards; however, experts stress that a legitimate organization will never ask a customer to pay with a gift card.

Most people do not have the technical skills to retaliate against scammers, but the potential victim in Browning's video made common, avoidable mistakes that allowed the phishing fraudster to engage in blackmail. The scam was initiated with the typical phishing bait. The victim received an email with a phony receipt for $500 that allegedly was paid to renew a subscription for security software. The victim was aware that he had never ordered the software, so he called the tech support number in the email to get a refund. This was the mark's first mistake. The phone call connected him to a scam call center in India. A man who sounded very helpful said he could deposit the refund directly into the victim's bank account. The victim committed another glaring mistake at this point by logging into his bank. This allowed the scammer to take control of the account.

Security experts say the best way to avoid phishing scams is to stop them before they start. Ignore all emails, texts, and voicemails from unknown senders, especially those that mention software that was never purchased. Delete suspicious messages immediately and block the senders. Do not click on any links in emails or texts, and never call phone numbers in suspicious messages. Anyone unsure about the source of a message should carefully inspect the email address; scammers usually use Gmail accounts, whereas real tech companies do not. Never give anyone personal information by phone, text, or email. Legitimate companies and government agencies never ask for passwords, complete social security numbers, or other sensitive data.

Do not be fooled by official-looking logos, company names, and images in the messages. Any scammer with basic skills in website design can steal the colors, fonts, logos, and other markers from genuine company websites and use them to create scam messages. If there are any questions about a bill, virus warning, or other problem, go directly to the official website of the company mentioned in the message. If you have an account, you can sign in and check your billing status and receive updates. If you do not have an account, you know the message is a phishing scam.

Scammers pretending to be customer tech support personnel often try to convince victims to go to the nearest store to purchase gift cards. In Browning's video, the scammer was on the phone with the victim walking him through the process of purchasing gift cards at a 7-Eleven. The victim was instructed to scratch off the security film on the back of the card and read the scammer the numbers. This would allow the scammer to retrieve the value of the card or resell it. Cybercriminals love gift cards because they are untraceable, and there is often no way for victims to get their money back.

Be aware that lawful businesses, especially international tech companies, do not allow customers to pay bills with gift cards. According to cybersecurity expert Jonathan Couch, "There are no legitimate reasons to give someone else a gift card as part of any legitimate transaction apart from a holiday or birthday, especially someone you don't know."[9] The same logic applies to Western Union or MoneyGram wire transfers. Legitimate organizations rarely, if ever, ask consumers to pay with wire transfers.

Anyone with an internet connection can be on the receiving end of a cyberattack. And no target is too big or influential to escape the demands of cybercriminals. Computer masterminds with bad intent will always find ways to separate victims from their money.

Diet and Health Scams

In the early 1990s, the internet was often referred to as the information superhighway. But in the twenty-first century it might be more accurate to call the internet the misinformation superhighway. Digital and social media are rife with conspiracy theories, fake news, and a relentless flood of bogus health and diet plans meant to confuse and deceive the public.

Alex Jones is one of the best-known conspiracy theorists traveling the misinformation superhighway. Jones runs the Infowars website, where visitors can find dozens of alarming stories that would be horrible if true. According to Jones, a secretive government entity called the "Deep State" is working to destroy the United States from within. After almost every mass shooting, Infowars pushes the baseless idea that the massacre was a hoax; the victims were all paid actors hired by the government to justify strict gun control laws. Infowars publishes misleading articles and doctored photos and videos that are used to attack immigrants, liberals, and members of the LGBTQ+ community. Jones repeatedly makes baseless claims about the origins of COVID-19 and the lack of safety and effectiveness of vaccines used to prevent the disease.

Jones repeats his unfounded theories on the *Alex Jones Show* podcast. After nearly two decades on the air, Jones was finally banned from almost every social media site in

> "[Alex Jones is part of the] wellness-conspiracy industrial complex. . . . When people click on the stories and land on his site, they are bombarded with ads for snake oil."[10]
>
> —Farhad Manjoo, journalist

the late 2010s, including Apple, Facebook, YouTube, and Spotify, for peddling misinformation. Despite the bans, Jones continues to earn around $55 million annually by selling costly health and wellness supplements and other merchandise. Although Jones can no longer advertise on most social media platforms, he was still selling his products in 2023 from his Infowars Store on Amazon. Journalist Farhad Manjoo claims, "[Jones is part of the] wellness-conspiracy industrial complex. Jones produces an incessant barrage of outrageous, thinly sourced or wholly mendacious content in the hopes that some of it will go viral. When people click on the stories and land on his site, they are bombarded with ads for snake oil [bogus health products]."[10]

Alex Jones is shown addressing demonstrators at a 2020 rally in Texas, where he is protesting COVID-19 stay-at-home orders. Using his Infowars website, Jones has made many false statements about this illness.

Marketing Schemes on TikTok

Anyone looking at TikTok for more than a few minutes will likely see videos posted by young women bragging about their weight loss. Some of the influencers push sketchy products such as skinny coffee, fat-fighter pills, and diet gummies. Viewers hoping to achieve the same results might be instructed to text a message containing a hashtag, number, or a phrase. This takes them to a website that promises a great new way to earn money selling diet products. While promising employment, the website is promoting a sales tactic known as multilevel marketing (MLM), or a pyramid scheme.

In 2022 an MLM company called It Works was being promoted by health and wellness influencers on TikTok, Instagram, and Facebook. It Works, like all MLM companies, signs up individuals to work as distributors. Distributors are required to spend hundreds of dollars every month to buy It Works diet products. Although distributors might make a small profit reselling the products, It Works pushes them to recruit their friends and family as new distributors. This often proves to be an impossible task. While the main company gets rich off distributor purchases, most MLM distributors typically waste time and money, with little to show for their efforts.

Desperate for Diets

Jones is one of many media personalities hawking unproven, alternative treatments that are linked to political views that insist there are alternative facts. Others include televangelist Jim Bakker, lawyer Rudy Giuliani, and podcaster Candace Owens. Another sector of the online health scam industry might be called the diet influencer industrial complex. Influencers ranging from movie and television stars to so-called mommy bloggers, or momfluencers, can be found on social media sites promoting risky or ineffective diet treatments.

Diet influencers far outnumber those in the "wellness-conspiracy" business—and it is easy to see why. According to the Boston Medical Center, two-thirds of Americans are overweight or obese. Around 45 million plan to go on a diet at any given time. This has created a $33 billion annual market for weight-loss treatments.

There are thousands of health and fitness influencers on TikTok, Instagram, and other social media sites. They post countless photos and videos of their healthy meals, workout routines,

> "Some weight loss supplements are laced with the now-banned appetite suppressant sibutramine. And weight loss . . . supplements might contain dangerous, prohibited amphetamine-like stimulants."[11]
>
> —Pieter Cohen, physician and Harvard University professor of medicine

and toned, tanned bodies. Although some offer legitimate advice, others are paid to promote weight-loss products such as diet shakes, detox teas, and appetite suppressant lollipops. These goods are often ineffective, and some contain dangerous, banned, or even illegal ingredients, according to Pieter Cohen, a physician and Harvard University professor of medicine. "Some weight loss supplements are laced with the now-banned appetite suppressant sibutramine," he writes. "And weight loss . . . supplements might contain dangerous, prohibited amphetamine-like stimulants."[11] These dangerous ingredients do not help users lose weight, but they can cause adverse effects, including irregular heartbeat, dizziness, and even strokes and heart attacks.

Fad Followers

Whereas some influencers sell dangerous or worthless pills, others promote diet hacks. These fads are sold as simple-sounding tricks that can supposedly improve health or fool the body into losing weight with little effort. In 2022 the concept of gut health blew up on TikTok, where the videos tagged with *#guttok* attracted more than 500 million views. The gut health trend spawned thousands of videos promoting questionable treatments.

Gut is a term used to describe the gastrointestinal tract—digestive organs that include the stomach and intestines. The gut has bacteria and hormones that process food and waste. People with bad gut health experience constipation, bloating, and other problems. Doctors recommend improving gut health by avoiding junk food and eating whole grains, fruits, vegetables, and bacteria-rich foods such as yogurt. Influencers on TikTok have their own ideas, however. Bria Lemirande, who has more than 1.8 million followers on Instagram and TikTok, recommends drinking several ounces of aloe vera juice every day to improve gut health.

Another influencer, "oliveoilqueen," who has nearly 30 million followers, lives up to her screen name by telling her followers to drink several shots of raw olive oil every day. Others recommend ingesting boiled apples, cucumber-ginger juice, and sweet potato soup to improve gut health. Some of the most popular TikTok videos feature "before" photos of a bloated, swollen gut and "after" photos of a nice, smooth stomach.

Social media influencers jump on wellness fads because they know that their videos, photos, and hashtags can attract millions of clicks, likes, and followers. This helps them earn money from sponsors who pay them to promote their products. Like Alex Jones, some social media stars market their own line of products to fans. Yet although promoting diet fads might be great for influencers, those who follow their advice might be harming

A fitness influencer talks about supplements. Some influencers promote goods that contain ineffective, dangerous, or even illegal ingredients.

themselves. Drinking excessive amounts of aloe vera juice or olive oil can cause stomachache, diarrhea, and other intestinal problems. Research shows that long-term lifestyle habits can improve gut health, but the so-called hacks are mainly about bowel movements. Gastroenterologist Rabia De Latour says, "That's what people are referring to when they say gut health. . . . They want to stamp a nice, pretty name on it, but it's about pooping."[12] And, though the images might suggest it, improving bowel health does not lead to trimmer waistlines.

Diet and detox teas, which are sold as weight-loss products, are based on the same logic; the products drastically increase bowel movements. Drinks with names such as FitTea, SkinnyMe Tea, and Bootea have been promoted by powerful influencers, including the Kardashian-Jenner family and rapper Cardi B.

Ads for diet and detox teas use terms such as *slimming* and *flat tummy*, but the main ingredient in most of these teas is an herb

Fake Celebrity Endorsements

Not everyone can attract millions of followers to their social media posts. But anyone can create a blizzard of clicks and likes by impersonating a celebrity. In 2022, scammers were selling bogus weight-loss gummies using talk show celebrity Oprah Winfrey as clickbait. One Facebook ad, viewed more than 120,000 times, said "Grab Your Fitness-Gummy From Oprah! . . . Just three weeks in, and she already melted off 100 [pounds]." The ad was followed by a Facebook video that showed footage of Winfrey and other celebrities. Their images were mixed into a video collage that featured piles of candy gummy bears and anonymous young women modeling their thin bodies and jumping for joy.

Those who took the clickbait were taken to a website to buy fitness gummies. The website contained a fake article from *Time* magazine that falsely claimed the gummies were created by Winfrey in a partnership with the Weight Watchers diet company. Although Winfrey is famous for her weight loss journey over the years, she was never associated with any type of weight-loss supplement. According to a Winfrey spokesperson, "These ads are a complete fabrication. Oprah has nothing to do with this gummy product and does not endorse any such diet or weight-loss pill."

Quoted in Bayliss Wagner, "Fact Check: Ads Claiming to Sell Oprah Winfrey Weight-Loss Gummies Are Scams," *USA Today*, May 31, 2022. www.usatoday.com.

known as senna, an extremely powerful laxative. Senna is used by doctors to treat constipation and to clear the intestines before colonoscopy diagnostic tests. Senna causes temporary water weight loss by sending users to the bathroom more often. Although social media influencers might look beautiful and perfectly composed when posing with a package of diet tea on Instagram, those who ingest senna experience stomach cramps, diarrhea, and the inability to control their bowels. Drinking diet teas on a regular basis is extremely unhealthy. The body does not properly absorb nutrients and calories from food. And senna can cause the intestines to become dependent on it. Once stopped, this can lead to constipation, bloating, and, ironically, weight gain. Additionally, the teas have been blamed for unplanned pregnancies; the laxative effect prevents the proper absorption of birth control pills.

Body Anxiety

In addition to senna, most diet and detox teas contain high amounts of caffeine. This ingredient is falsely said to speed up the metabolism. This allegedly helps the body burn more calories, leading to weight loss. But caffeine can cause sleeplessness, tremors, irritability, and a high heart rate. Too much caffeine can also cause anxiety, and many of those who seek diet advice on social media are already anxious. According to an internal survey by Instagram, leaked to the public in 2021, the app worsened body image issues in one out of three teen girls. One female British user mentioned in the study explains, "You can't ever win on social media. If you're curvy, you're too busty. If you're skinny, you're too skinny. If you're bigger, you're too fat. But it's clear you need . . . to be thin, to be pretty. It's endless, and you just end up feeling worthless."[13]

The report generated intense criticism of Instagram in 2021, but studies show that harmful dieting and eating disorder hashtags are also in abundance on TikTok, one of the most popular sites in the world with users between the ages of sixteen and twenty-four. And with more than half a billion female users worldwide, TikTok attracts a wide range of ads for weight loss products that are unhealthy and do not work as promised.

TikTok has an official policy that bans ads for fasting apps and weight-loss supplements that promote a harmful or negative body image. However, sellers have eluded the ban by promoting their products as part of a healthful or mindful diet. Researchers blame TikTok's "For You" page, where artificial intelligence algorithms recommend videos based on a user's history. Within minutes, analysts who searched for diet-related content were shown videos that promoted unhealthy fasting regimens, unproven appetite suppressants, and extreme weight-loss programs. Critics say videos sponsoring scam diets and products are only part of the problem with TikTok. The site's augmented reality camera filters also promote a negative body message. There are dozens of filters on the site that allow users to change the appearance of their skin, face, and body shape. This allows influencers to promote impossible standards of beauty among young girls who mistakenly accept such standards as ideal.

Disease Disinformation

Scammers selling bogus products are skilled in taking advantage of people's insecurities. After the COVID-19 pandemic swept across the globe in 2020, an entire new industry was created to exploit public fears. With most people stuck at home during the early days of the pandemic, supposed miracle cures or preventative treatments for COVID-19 flooded social media. And the scams continued long after safe and effective COVID-19 vaccines were introduced in early 2021.

A June 2021 report from the Center for Countering Digital Hate (CCDH) discovered that 65 percent of the online anti-vaccine disinformation could be traced to just twelve people. Disinformation is misinformation that is intentionally spread to mislead the public. The CCDH labeled these anti-vaxxers the "Disinformation Dozen." Members of this group, many of whom remain active on social media, state without evidence that COVID-19 vaccines have numerous harmful side effects. Most of those in the Disinformation Dozen sell expensive nutritional supplements they claim can prevent or treat the disease.

A Florida osteopath named Joseph Mercola is a significant figure in the Disinformation Dozen. Anyone who searches for coronavirus information can easily find articles posted by Mercola that contain disinformation. Mercola wrongly asserts that COVID-19 vaccines alter the deoxyribonucleic acid (DNA) of those who receive the shots. Most people are familiar with the double helix spiral of DNA, long molecules that comprise genes. DNA is often compared to a set of blueprints, a recipe, or a code that determines a person's physical features, such as gender and hair and eye color. The COVID-19 vaccine has been extensively studied, and there is no evidence that it alters DNA. However, Mercola falsely claims that altered DNA caused by vaccines will "destroy the lives of millions."[14]

Mercola does not work alone; he employs numerous writers who, by 2022, had produced more than six hundred anti-vax

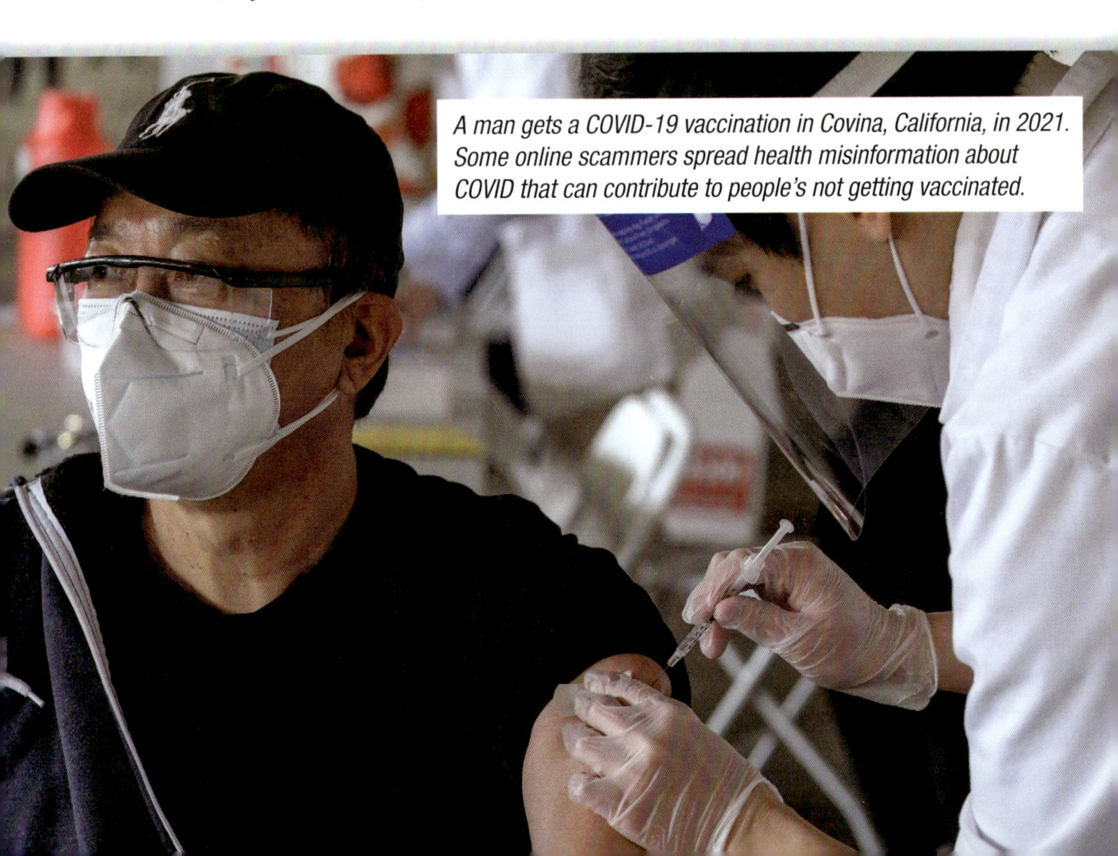

A man gets a COVID-19 vaccination in Covina, California, in 2021. Some online scammers spread health misinformation about COVID that can contribute to people's not getting vaccinated.

articles published in more than a dozen languages. In that year, Mercola had more than 1.7 million followers on his main Facebook page. Facebook has labeled some of the content on Mercola's page as false and removed several articles for violating Facebook policy. But researchers have tied Mercola to at least seventeen Facebook accounts that were connected to his business. And although the claims he publishes are not based on facts, Mercola's words have been copied, quoted, and shared by influencers, bloggers, and anti-vax activists on social media platforms throughout the world.

A 2022 research study sponsored by several universities, including Stanford and New York University, called Mercola a pseudomedical influencer, or PMI. People in this category use their medical credentials to undermine legitimate scientific research. Like many PMIs, Mercola sells a wide range of nutritional supplements and other products on his website. He has stated in the past that he is worth more than $100 million.

Rebuff Diet and Health Rip-Offs

One way to avoid diet and health scams is to understand that the majority of supplements are untested and unnecessary. Most people get all their necessary vitamins and minerals from the foods they eat. And many of the claims made by supplement producers are not accurate. The US Food and Drug Administration (FDA), which oversees health products, can levy fines against those who claim their vitamins, minerals, and herbs will cure a disease or prevent a viral infection. But influencers selling wellness products often make sketchy claims that skirt the formal regulations. A seller, for example, can say that a product improves cognitive functions or burns fat. Scammers might also use words meant to give consumers the impression that their products are safe and effective. But terms such as *clinically proven, breakthrough treatment, backed by science,* or *laboratory tested* have little real meaning. The claims rarely cite a laboratory, clinic, or scientific study that proves their statements. Despite the misleading claims, influencers can be very convincing. As Pieter Cohen explains, "Because of the way social media is, it's very easy to link testimonials or little posts or tweets with things that will suggest to consumers . . . that this product will be able to treat their [problem]."[15]

Around half of all Americans take supplements, but Cohen, a Harvard-based physician, says a very small percentage are tested for safety or effectiveness by the FDA. If you do want to try a supplement, consult the dietary supplement fact sheets produced by the National Institutes of Health. These provide unbiased information about health, diet, and wellness products. If you do decide to purchase a vitamin, herb, or mineral, avoid websites run by influencers, conspiracy theorists, and podcasters. These sites usually sell products for about twice as much as they cost at a local drugstore or on an e-commerce website.

Another way to avoid wellness scams is to assume that trending diet fads are worthless and might even be dangerous. As weight loss specialist Malia Frey writes, no diet drink, pill, or powder will take off the pounds: "As much as we hate to admit it, most of us know that the best way to lose weight and maintain the weight loss is to use old-fashioned common sense methods. Sustainable weight loss takes time. . . . Choose nutritious foods, eat mindfully, and find physical activity that you enjoy and can be consistent with. Focus on your health first, and never put yourself at risk."[16]

Truth and Lies

Online scammers will latch on to any fad, tragedy, or rumor to promote their products. While they are making money selling dummy cures, these wellness fraudsters are also creating widespread problems. According to digital literacy expert Megan Marrelli, "It's easy to forget that health misinformation, including about Covid, can still contribute to people not getting vaccinated. . . . We know for a fact that health misinformation contributes to the spread of real-world disease."[17]

> "We know for a fact that health misinformation contributes to the spread of real-world disease."[17]
>
> —Megan Marrelli, digital literacy expert

Members of the diet and wellness community claim to be acting in the public's best interest. But the toxic material they post can harm the people they claim to be helping. And tamping down the scams is nearly impossible. Twitter, Facebook, YouTube, and other platforms have taken down hundreds of thousands of posts that violate their policies on health, diet, and disease misinformation. But people continue to trust influencers and others who market simple, easy solutions to complex health and diet problems. Although fraudsters often craft persuasive arguments and social media sites can amplify false claims, researching these assertions and locating reputable sources will quickly reveal the biased and deceptive practices and help people avoid falling for them in the future.

Crypto and Financial Fraud

In 2022 Sam Bankman-Fried was often described in the press as a financial rock star with a net worth of $26 billion. The boyish thirty-year-old, known as SBF, was famous for his tangled, messy hairdo and unkempt appearance. He earned his billions as a founder of FTX, one of the world's largest cryptocurrency exchanges.

Millions of investors used the FTX exchange to buy and sell digital cryptocurrency. Crypto is created using complex encryption algorithms that make it possible to transfer funds between individuals. Crypto coins, called tokens, are promoted as alternative forms of payment, but the value of cryptocurrency fluctuates constantly. Anyone can create cryptocurrency; it is valued at whatever investors are willing to pay for the tokens. FTX minted its own cryptocurrency, called FTT. Part of Bankman-Fried's wealth was based on his digital stockpile of FTT tokens, which were worth more than $80 each in 2021.

With the success of FTX, Bankman-Fried was featured on the covers of business magazines such as *Forbes* and *Fortune.* His financial genius was the subject of articles in the *New York Times,* on the website Vox, and via other prominent media. Journalists were especially captivated by SBF's noble view of wealth; he promised to give away most of his profits to those in need.

"The most essential gift of a con man is that they can inspire trust that never wavers, even in the face of red flags and worrisome details."[18]

—Diana Henriques, financial historian

In November 2022 Bankman-Fried's fortune evaporated when FTX filed for bankruptcy and the FTT token lost most of its value. Although FTX had been widely promoted as a safe and secure online crypto trading platform, that belief was based on lies cultivated by Bankman-Fried. He was not a financial genius. Like every other successful con man, Bankman-Fried was a good salesman who gained the confidence of his marks with slick talk about a complex financial scheme that would make them rich. Financial historian Diana Henriques writes, "The most essential gift of a con man is that they can inspire trust that never wavers, even in the face of red flags and worrisome details. You can't look at FTX as anything but a massive leap of faith by a lot of people who should have known better."[18]

Sam Bankman-Fried (on right) is shown on his way to a court hearing in Manhattan in January 2023. He was indicted on eight felony counts for his crypto scheme, which has been called the biggest financial fraud in US history.

Bankman-Fried used investor funds to support a lavish lifestyle. He purchased property worth $121 million on an island in the Bahamas called New Providence, where he resided in a $30 million penthouse. Bankman-Fried met with politicians, celebrities, and respected financial experts, many of whom invested in his scheme. But according to charges by the US Securities and Exchange Commission (SEC), which enforces financial regulations, "Bankman-Fried was orchestrating a massive, yearslong fraud, diverting billions of dollars of the trading platform's customer funds for his own personal benefit and to help grow his crypto empire."[19] Bankman-Fried was indicted on eight felony counts that could send him to prison for the rest of his life. His crypto scheme has been called the biggest financial fraud in US history. Those who bought FTT tokens lost all their money.

New Trends, Old Tricks

Cryptocurrency is an unregulated financial tool so complex that few people really understand how it works. This makes crypto extremely attractive to scammers. Tech writer Amanda Hetler agrees: "Where money is concerned, scams always follow. And the same is true with cryptocurrency. . . . [And] even though cryptocurrency is a newer trend, thieves are using old methods to steal."[20]

One of these methods relies on the old-school con man trick of impersonating a successful investment manager. In the past, these phony financial experts would promise their targets they could make money by investing in precious metals, oil wells, real estate, or some other get-rich-quick scheme. Today the most popular cons involve crypto. Swindlers posing as investment managers promise victims that if they pay a fee to initiate the deal, they will make big bucks. Sometimes the scammer asks for a bank account number

"Where money is concerned, scams always follow. . . . Even though cryptocurrency is a newer trend, thieves are using old methods to steal."[20]

—Amanda Hetler, tech writer

under the guise of transferring future profits to the mark. Once the fees are paid and the sensitive personal information is obtained, the scammer ghosts the victim.

Fake websites are popular with all types of scammers, including those engaged in financial fraud. Legitimate-looking sites display logos and photos of a real bank or financial firm. The sites might also feature fake endorsements from trusted celebrities. This deception is meant to create feelings of security and trust while trapping investors in scams.

Pulling the Rug Out from Under Investors

The rug pull, or exit scam, is another old-fashioned fraud that has been repurposed with a high-tech twist. In the past, exit scammers would set up a phony company, take orders from the public, and never ship the products. The swindlers would disappear, or exit, before victims discovered that they were robbed. Crypto rug pull scams require much less work. Cybercriminals create a crypto token using software that is readily available online. The scammers create a buzz around the token on social media, sometimes using fake celebrity endorsements. Con artists might also create phony articles and marketing reports that show their crypto coin is about to explode in value. If enough people buy into the hype, the price of the token climbs. This attracts more investors until a large amount of money is accumulated in a type of digital bank account called a liquidity pool. Scammers then pull the rug out from under investors: they siphon the money from the liquidity pool into their own bank accounts. This causes the value of the coin to plummet, leaving investors with nothing.

Like most online scammers, rug pullers are quick to exploit the latest fads. That is how the hit South Korean television thriller *Squid Game* inspired one of the costliest rug pull rip-offs in history. In 2021 *Squid Game* was the number one Netflix show in ninety-four countries, including the United States. The show revolves around people who have large debts. They play children's

Fine Print Rip-Off

Cryptocurrencies are not regulated by the Securities and Exchange Commission or any other government entity. This means scammers can sometimes rip off crypto investors without violating any law. Around six hundred thousand Americans learned this in 2022 when the cryptocurrency lending company Celsius Network declared bankruptcy. Celsius offered crypto savings accounts that were similar to those provided by a traditional bank; people deposited their crypto into accounts and earned interest on the deposit. Whereas legitimate banks were paying 1 to 3 percent interest on savings accounts in 2022, Celsius offered annual interest rates of up to 20 percent on crypto deposits.

Like many crypto scammers, Celsius founder Alex Mashinsky cultivated the image of a know-it-all financial wizard who charmed millions of followers on Twitter and YouTube. After Celsius imploded in 2022, depositors found they could not withdraw their crypto from their savings accounts. They had failed to read the lengthy contract, called terms of use, that most websites publish but few consumers bother to read. The terms of use clearly stated that all cryptocurrency deposits became the sole property of the Celsius Network. When Celsius declared bankruptcy, depositors' crypto assets legally became Mashinsky's property.

games such as tug-of-war to win millions in prize money. Those who lose are brutally murdered.

The *Squid Game* rug pullers devised a clever setup. They claimed that they were launching an online game based on the show. Anyone who wanted to play would have to buy Squid tokens (SQUID), a pay-to-play cryptocurrency minted by the swindlers. The developers created a fear-of-missing-out buzz around the game; the project's Twitter and Telegram accounts had a combined total of 128,000 followers. When SQUID was made available to the public, it sold out in one second. The value of the token soared 23 million percent in six days, from around one cent to more than $2,861.

Red Flags Ignored

The SQUID surge attracted uncritical international media attention from the BBC, CNBC, and other networks. Most stories failed to mention that the SQUID token and online game were never approved by Netflix or the creators of the *Squid Game* television show. In fact, the token's developers were illegally using the show's trademarks and copyrighted material. Some online financial experts did try to issue warnings. Crypto specialists cautioned that SQUID came out of nowhere and seemed too good to be true. Crypto analyst Brooke Becher writes, "This list of red flags begins with unknown or anonymous project leaders, a barren, low-quality website and a guarantee of high returns. Lofty goals to be completed in an unreasonably short timeframe . . . [decorate the] start-up's homepage, accompanied by suspicious social media activity, littered with buzzwords and a desperate sense of urgency."[21] Additionally, those who promoted SQUID misspelled words and used clunky English phrases, something that is associated with scammers operating from Russia or other foreign countries. The warnings went unheeded by many eager crypto investors.

The Netflix show Squid Game, *pictured here, inspired one of the costliest "rug pull" rip-offs in history. The scam defrauded victims of more than $3.3 million.*

Elon Musk and Dogecoin

Elon Musk, founder of the Tesla automotive company and the aerospace giant SpaceX, is one of the richest people on Earth. In late 2020 Musk spoke highly of the cryptocurrency token Dogecoin, which had a value of less than one cent. Musk began promoting Dogecoin to his 45 million Twitter followers, tweeting messages such as "Dogecoin is the people's crypto." Financial experts say that Musk's tweets helped attract interest to Dogecoin, which soared to 74 cents by early May.

As Dogecoin was reaching record highs, Musk appeared as a guest on the sketch comedy show *Saturday Night Live.* In one sketch, Musk called Dogecoin a hustle. This caused a panicked sell-off among Dogecoin holders. Within an hour of Musk's appearance, the token had lost 20 percent of its value. A few days later it was trading at less than six cents. Some analysts believe Musk purchased around $382 million worth of Dogecoins at a rock-bottom price in 2020. He is thought to have sold his holdings before he appeared on television. Crypto analysts believe he made over $9.4 billion from Dogecoin. In 2022 Musk was sued for $285 billion by a group of Dogecoin holders who lost money after the value of the coin crashed.

Quoted in Chris Isidore, "Elon Musk Tweeted. Dogecoin Surged More than 50%," CNN, February 4, 2021. www.cnn.com.

After the price of SQUID skyrocketed, the rug pullers cleaned out the liquidity pool, making off with more than $3.3 million. Within ten minutes, SQUID was worthless, trading at one-third of one cent. One anonymous investor said he bought $5,000 worth of SQUID: "I lost all of what I had in this project."[22] After the crash, rug pullers released a statement dripping with irony, blaming outsiders for the crash. "Someone is trying to hack our project these days," the notification read. "Squid Game [Developer] does not want to continue running the project as we are depressed from the scammers and [are] overwhelmed with stress."[23]

It is easy to understand why the SQUID scam is called a rug pull: when someone has the rug pulled out from under them, they fall hard. But investors keep falling for rug pulls. According to the cryptocurrency research company Chainalysis, rug pulls accounted for 37 percent of all crypto scams in 2021, compared to 1 percent the previous year. In total, rug pulls cost cryptocurrency investors more than $2.8 billion, or $7 million a day. And most rug pulls are designed to target innocent marks. As Becher writes, "Rug pulls are decked out in bells and whistles—a trail of social media hype and fancy graphics designed to bamboozle inexperienced investors."[24]

Pump and Dump

Another old-style con refashioned for the modern era is known as the pump and dump. The scam is similar in some ways to the rug pull, except pump and dump schemes usually involve financial instruments called securities, such as stocks and bonds. People have been running pump and dump scams in the United States since the nineteenth century. The only major change is that social media is used to run the con.

In 2022, eight influencers were arrested in a multimillion-dollar pump and dump scheme carried out on Twitter and Discord. The defendants posed as successful stock traders in trading chatrooms, where they attracted hundreds of thousands of followers. The swindlers purchased stocks and promoted them to others, causing the prices to climb. When the prices did rise, the scammers dumped their holdings. This triggered a massive sell-off that caused the value of the stocks to plunge. According to Joseph Sansone, chief of the SEC Enforcement Division,

> The defendants used social media to amass a large following of novice investors and then took advantage of their followers by repeatedly feeding them a steady diet of misinformation, which resulted in fraudulent profits of approximately $100 million. Today's action exposes the true motivation of these alleged fraudsters and serves as another warning that investors should be wary of unsolicited advice they encounter online.[25]

Those who engage in securities pump and dump schemes can be charged with serious crimes. Felonies include securities fraud and wire fraud, which makes it illegal to use radio, television, or the internet to execute a pump and dump scheme. But the SEC does not regulate cryptocurrency. This means there are no laws against pumping up a crypto token on social media and dumping it when the price peaks.

Do Not Gamble on Cryptocurrency

Crypto scams occur every day throughout the world. The Africrypt rug pull bilked South Africans out of $3.6 billion in 2021. The Gain-Bitcoin scam stole $4.7 billion from people in India. Other billion-dollar cons occurred in England and South Korea. With so much money readily available to criminals, crypto scams are likely to continue. FBI agent George L. Piro remarks, "The technology has changed, but the crime remains the same. Unscrupulous fraudsters are nothing new to the investment world—what's changing is they are now pushing their criminal activity into the cryptocurrency

A woman uses her phone to check the price of Bitcoin. Financial experts say cryptocurrency is a bad investment.

> "The technology has changed, but the crime remains the same. . . . Investors beware. Conduct your due diligence before investing."[26]
>
> —George L. Piro, FBI agent

realm. Investors beware. Conduct your due diligence before investing."[26]

Financial experts say cryptocurrency is a bad investment even if buyers manage to avoid the thousands of scams surrounding digital currency. The value of a crypto coin can skyrocket one day and plunge the next. For example, the most popular cryptocurrency, Bitcoin, moved from around $5,000 in 2020 to over $64,000 in 2021. Several months later, it was worth only $16,000.

In 2021 a study by the Bank for International Settlements showed that 80 percent of global investors lost money on cryptocurrency investments when Bitcoin crashed and dragged all other crypto tokens down with it. Those who lost money apparently failed to understand that speculating on any cryptocurrency is little different than gambling in a casino. Actor and outspoken crypto skeptic Ben McKenzie says, "I've always placed crypto somewhere between pointless and a scam."[27]

McKenzie is not just talking about scammers stealing cryptocurrency. In his view, the entire crypto concept is a scam. Big investors make money when they convince others to buy the tokens. The system only works as long as people are willing to buy the coins. When they stop buying, prices plunge. McKenzie says that the best way to avoid crypto scams is to simply avoid buying into the system: "Cryptocurrencies are not actually currencies by any reasonable economic definition. They're a poor medium of exchange, a unit of account, and store of value. . . . And they're being sold in these unregulated marketplaces. So the propensity towards fraud is just sort of undeniable."[28]

Although some were lucky enough to buy low and sell high, many more lost money buying into the Bitcoin fad. Some who gambled on crypto lost their college funds, mortgage payments, and life savings hoping to get rich quickly. They would have been better off following the old gambling advice: never bet more than you can stand to lose.

Romance Rip-Offs

In 2022 a fifteen-year-old girl living in Riverside, California, thought she had found a perfect new boyfriend online. The boy, who said he was seventeen, seemed caring and sincere. As he cultivated a romantic relationship, the boy learned personal details about the girl, including her address. The girl ended the online relationship after the boy asked for nude photos. Days later, he was knocking on her front door.

The boy turned out to be Austin Lee Edwards, a twenty-eight-year-old sheriff's deputy from Virginia. Edwards drove across the country to kidnap the girl he met online. He shot and killed the girl's mother, grandmother, and grandfather, then set their house on fire. Edwards left with the girl and managed to elude police for several hours. As the cops closed in, he shot himself with the gun issued to him by the Virginia sheriff's department. Journalist Robin Abcarian picks up the story: "Police said the girl was unhurt, at least physically. Can you imagine, though, her emotional wounds?"[29]

The girl's name was withheld because she is a minor. But what happened to her could happen to anyone looking for romance online, young or old, male or female, straight or gay. The Riverside girl was catfished by a romance scammer. Catfishing occurs when a predator creates a false identity online, usually with stolen photos of a very attractive person.

"Love bombing is an attempt to influence or control someone through the use of (often disingenuous) attention and affection."[30]

—Sahana Prasad, sexual trauma therapist

Catfishers research their targets' social media feeds to learn their interests, hobbies, and friends. They are eager to text for hours with their victims to establish a close relationship. And romance scammers are always ready with a compliment or helpful suggestion. Many predators are experts at love bombing, a term commonly used on social media. According to sexual trauma therapist Sahana Prasad, "Love bombing is an attempt to influence or control someone through the use of (often disingenuous) attention and affection."[30] When catfishers love bomb, they manipulate their victims by making over-the-top declarations of love. Predators will strive to remain in constant communication with their targets. They quickly begin using mushy pet names like *my queen* or *my true love*. Scammers con their victims into making long-range plans, sometimes even proposing marriage after a few days.

After flooding their victim's inbox with love bomb texts day after day, catfishers launch their scam: they ask for inappropriate photos, money, expensive gifts, and personal information. If the target tries to break off the relationship, the predator might engage in "sextortion": they threaten to send embarrassing photos to friends and family unless the victim cooperates.

Sweetheart Scammers

Social media is full of people looking for love, and romance scammers are experts at exploiting the emotionally vulnerable. Con artists called sweetheart scammers target lonely older people who have experienced divorce or the loss of a spouse. Sweetheart scams are often conducted by men posing as women. One such case was reported in a Detroit suburb in 2022. An unnamed seventy-five-year-old man was drawn into an online relationship by someone posing on Instagram as a female professional wrestler. According to the victim, "She wanted to be with me. She wanted to come here and live with me. And she wanted to marry me. That's what she said."[31]

> "She wanted to be with me. She wanted to come here and live with me. And she wanted to marry me. That's what she said."[31]
>
> —An anonymous victim of a romance scam

The sweetheart scammer only communicated with the victim through emails and texts. The scammer claimed to have a large sum of money in a Florida bank, but she said someone had gained access to her account and it was therefore locked. The victim said, "I felt sorry for her. She was asking me if I could help her. She had a wrestling match coming up on the weekend. And I said I think I can probably help you. What do you need? She said, 'Well, I got to pay for the match. It's $200.'"[32]

Scammers often begin their cons by asking for a fairly small amount of money so they do not set off alarms with the intended target. In the Detroit case, the sweetheart scammer was soon requesting more money in the form of prepaid gift cards and Steam cards, which are used to pay for online video games and

A girl looks at her social media feed. Catfishers look at people's social media feeds to learn about their interests and friends, and then use that information to take advantage of those people.

The Case of Robert Blackwell

In 2022 the email security company Agari Cyber Intelligence Division investigated a romance scam ring called Scarlet Widow that operated out of Nigeria. Agari presented the case of Robert Blackwell to show "how intrusive and damaging these scams can be."

Blackwell had recently gone through a painful divorce in Texas. He met a phony fashion model called Laura Cahill, whose persona was created by Scarlet Widow. Laura claimed she had lost her credit cards and convinced Blackwell to wire her $1,700. Blackwell continued to give Laura money in hopes of cultivating a long-term relationship. The victim opened several bank accounts with large deposits and gave Laura access so she could withdraw funds electronically. When relatives told Blackwell he was being catfished, he said his relationship with Laura was part of God's plan. Blackwell went on to send the scammers over $50,000. At one point, he stole $10,000 from his stepfather to continue the relationship. After one year, Laura disappeared. According to Agari, "Laura Cahill's disappearance likely saved Robert from continuing to send her money, ultimately limiting the pain and suffering caused by the members of this exploitative group."

Agari Cyber Intelligence Division, *Scarlet Widow: Breaking Hearts for Profit*. Eden Prairie, MN: Agari, 2022. www.agari.com.

software. The requests for money kept coming until the man was out $80,000. After the victim ran out of money, he borrowed $5,000 from friends because he was desperate to remain in the relationship.

Romance Scammer Rings

Around one-quarter of adults sixty-five and older live alone and are considered socially isolated, according to the Centers for Disease Control and Prevention. Loneliness makes older people ripe targets for scammers. And swindlers can easily find vulnerable people seeking companionship on dating sites such as Dating 4 Disabled, SeniorMatch, and DivorcedPeopleMeet.com. These platforms provided dozens of victims for a romance scam ring called Scarlet Widow, which operated out of Nigeria until 2019. The scam was exposed by the email security company Agari Cyber Intelligence Division in 2022.

The Scarlet Widow gang followed the typical catfisher script when creating fake personas. They used made-up names and stolen pictures of attractive men and women. The scammers created dozens of fake accounts on social media and dating sites that featured similar messages. The phony love seekers all said they had experienced tragedy in the past but still believed in the power of love. According to the Agari report, "Each [account depicts] an alluring romantic partner—attractive, sensitive, and eager to find a life partner. Each one is also a fraud, custom-crafted to fill a gap in the life of a lonely heart, pry open their bank accounts, and heartlessly bleed them of every dollar they have—and then some."[33]

Scarlet Widow ran romance scams on men and women. The most successful fake persona, according to Agari, was a woman named Laura Cahill. Her fake account, which remained active on dating sites for two years, featured stolen photos ripped from the social media profile of a real fashion model. The Laura Cahill profile attracted dozens of men. Scarlet Widow scammers answered their inquiries using scripted templates designed to gain the trust of their targets. Laura said she was in Paris for a modeling seminar but would soon be back in the United States. She said she believed in open communication and treating others the way she wanted to be treated. But some of the responses should have raised red flags because they sounded like they were written by Nigerian scammers: "[I] have several pairs of shoes. . . . I use facial cleansers at times, Lotions and eye creams. I generally don't smell."[34]

Despite the silly language, "Laura" found plenty of victims. Once they were on the hook, the typical romance scam was initiated. The Laura template contained a long, detailed paragraph describing how someone had stolen her identity while she was in Paris. She could no longer use her credit cards. She begged her targets to wire her money through Western Union so she could buy a plane ticket home. If the target refused, she provided a contact with a travel agent who could confirm her story. The travel agent was part of the scam. If the mark believed the agent's story and sent the money, he would receive a fake confirmation that the ticket was purchased. Scarlet Widow obtained these confirmations by booking real flights, then canceling them. Of course, Laura never arrived in the United States. But she continued to exploit the victim for as long as possible, offering a range of excuses spelled out in various templates.

Romance scammer rings are known to operate out of Nigeria, Ghana, England, and Canada, though they can pop up anywhere. Agari confirms,

> These groups are methodical, operating like professional sales organizations, gathering prospects, using scripts to move toward the sale, managing numerous scams in parallel, and putting in the long-term investment of time needed to squeeze the maximum cash out of each victim. Once the victim is no longer useful to the gang, they drop all communication, ultimately leaving the victims alone and without the answers they crave.[35]

The Tinder Swindler

For obvious reasons, many victims of romance scams never video chat or meet their phony love interests in person. But the audacious Israeli con man Simon Leviev was able to carry on multiple romance scams that included face-to-face dates, vacations, and even arrangements to move in together.

In 2018 Leviev was posing as a billionaire heir to a diamond fortune. Leviev created a detailed online persona that portrayed him as the CEO of a company called LLD Diamonds. He backed this fiction with flashy photos that showed him wearing expensive designer clothes, riding in luxury cars, and traveling on a private jet with a fearsome-looking bodyguard.

When a twenty-nine-year-old Norwegian grad student named Cecilie Fjellhøy began exchanging messages with Leviev on the dating app Tinder, she was impressed. Fjellhøy was living in London at the time, and her first lunch date with Leviev was at the ex-

Simon Leviev is brought to court in Athens, Greece, in 2019. Leviev perpetrated multiple romance scams.

pensive Four Seasons Hotel. Fjellhøy recalled her first impression: "He has this magnetism. . . . There's something about this guy that is special."[36] Over lunch, Leviev said he needed to leave right away on a business trip to Bulgaria. He asked Fjellhøy if she was interested in traveling with him on his private jet. Fjellhøy was infatuated, but before she said yes, she googled her date. His story seemed to check out; everything she found online seemed to prove that Leviev was the son of a Russian Israeli diamond merchant.

Fjellhøy and Leviev began a whirlwind romance. Leviev constantly texted sweet messages to her and hinted at marriage during video chats. He sent her flowers and expensive gifts and

LGBTQ+ Extortion Scams

In 2022 the FTC reported that scammers were targeting people on LGBTQ+ dating apps such as Grindr and Feeld. These were not typical romance scams in which a con artist professes love and asks for money. Instead, the scammers were quick to send explicit photos to the victim while requesting similar photos in return. If the victim responded, the scammer threatened to show the photos to friends, family, or employers unless they were sent money or gift cards. This is called extortion or "sextortion." Sometimes scammers threaten people who are closeted—that is, their friends and family do not know they are LGBTQ+. The predator bullies the victims, promising to ruin their lives by revealing the explicit photos and conversations.

The FTC sited examples of sextortion perpetrators, including a Wisconsin scammer who was jailed for using Grindr to extort older married men who were closeted. Wisconsin assistant attorney general Annie Jay explains why sextortion is attractive to scammers: "The reason why it's effective as a blackmail scheme is the perpetrators rely on and choose victims who are less likely to report. There is an embarrassment angle inherent in the scheme."

Quoted in Katherine Skiba, "Sextortion Plaguing LGBTQ+ Dating Apps," AARP, December 21, 2021. www.aarp.org.

remembered her birthday. But Leviev stayed distant, claiming his job required him to travel constantly. The couple conducted most of their relationship online.

After three months, Fjellhøy received a troubling text. Leviev said his life was in danger. Nefarious enemies, possibly Russian mobsters, wanted to steal his fortune. Leviev backed up the claim with disturbing photos of himself and his bodyguard. They were bloodied, bruised, and bandaged after an alleged attack. Leviev said he was living in fear. He could not use his credit cards because they could be used by his enemies to track him down. Leviev initially asked Fjellhøy to lend him $25,000 so he could go into hiding. Seeing that her boyfriend was in danger, Fjellhøy had no problem borrowing the money. She recalls, "You didn't even think that it was a problem when you were taking up the loans because you were so sure that this guy . . . was part of the LLD Diamonds and that the money existed [to pay you back]."[37]

> "You didn't even think that it was a problem when you were taking up the loans because you were so sure that . . . the money existed [to pay you back]."[37]
>
> —Cecilie Fjellhøy, victim of romance scam

Leviev continued to ask for more money to maintain his luxurious lifestyle while in hiding. Fjellhøy took out loans and lines of credit and even flew suitcases full of cash to Leviev. She was soon $250,000 in debt. He continually promised to pay her back, telling her everything would be fine in a few weeks. When Fjellhøy was unable to make payments on the loans, she begged Leviev to send her money. He did send her small amounts. But checks for large sums bounced and wire transfers were promised but never seemed to go through. Leviev had dozens of excuses.

The Story Unravels

Fjellhøy did not know that she was one of at least three women Leviev was scamming at that time. They were all told the same story and shown the same photos that portrayed Leviev in grave danger. And all the women were borrowing huge sums of money to bail out their romantic partner. Leviev would take the money from one victim and use the funds to hook another victim with private jet trips and fancy hotels.

Fjellhøy finally realized she had been scammed. She told her story to a Norwegian newspaper to warn other potential victims. She soon met with the two other women who were being swindled by Leviev at the same time. With reporters on the story, Fjellhøy discovered that Leviev had been running his romance scam for years. His real name was Shimon Hayut. He had been sentenced to two years in jail in Finland in 2015 for defrauding women. He had also served time in Israel for passing bad checks.

By the time Fjellhøy ended the relationship, Leviev was wanted by authorities in Israel, Sweden, England, Germany, Denmark, and Norway. In 2019 he was arrested in Greece for using a fake passport. Leviev was sent back to Israel, but he only served five months in prison. According to the *Times of Israel,* Leviev may have stolen $10 million from victims between 2017 and 2019. In 2022 Fjellhøy told her story in the Netflix real-crime documentary *The Tinder Swindler,* directed by Felicity Morris. While Leviev was a free man at that time, Fjellhøy said she was still paying off their debts. As Morris said, "This isn't just catfishing—this is catfishing on a whole other level."[38]

Reject Romance Scammers

Average catfishers do not approach their romance rip-offs with Leviev's level of criminal skill and commitment. Most set off alarms that should have warned potential victims that they were being targeted. Journalist Adryan Corcione writes, "If you're at all suspicious that someone you're talking to online is not, in fact, who they say they are, you could be a victim of catfishing."[39]

Most catfishers use stolen identities that can be discovered by googling their name and conducting a reverse-image search with the profile photos they provide. Journalist Katelyn Burns suspected she was being catfished on the dating app OKCupid; her potential suitor sounded too good to be true. Burns says, "I did a reverse Google image search on his pictures and found a different guy's Facebook account. [The different guy's] only public post on the account was 'My account was hacked again.'"[40] When Burns saw that message, her suspicions were confirmed. A catfisher had stolen the man's Facebook photos and identity to run romance scams.

There are several other warning signs that a victim is being catfished. Often, romance scammers are men posing as women, so they will not participate in video chats. Most romance scammers also refuse to meet in person. Some make dates to string the victim along but cancel at the last minute, often with odd-sounding excuses. And, of course, the scammers are always after money, and they are quick to ask for cash. Sincere potential partners will rarely wheedle for gifts, loans, or airplane tickets within hours or days of meeting someone. Business journalist Kelvin Collins as-

A man looks at a dating app. Many people have found true love dating online, but romance scams are also common.

serts, "A good rule is to never send money to someone you've never met in person. Another good rule is to remember that someone who cares about you will not ask you to place yourself in financial jeopardy for them or put you in a difficult position."[41]

Collins also warns against revealing too much personal information in social media profiles. Do not list your financial situation, home address, phone number, or workplace in profiles where anyone can see them. Care should also be taken when posting photos; never share pictures that you would not want your friends, family, and employers to see. Photographs remain forever on the internet, and revealing or intimate pictures can be used to blackmail you.

Red Flags

Millions of people have found true love dating online, but the FTC calls romance scams a social media gold mine. According to the FTC, victims lost more than $547 million to catfishers in 2021 alone. That is more than six times the reported losses in 2017. And experts say the amount lost in romance scams is likely much higher: many mortified victims are too embarrassed to report the crime.

Like all swindles, the too-good-to-be-true rule applies to online romance. Wealthy diamond traders and fashion models are not likely to be found looking for love on a dating app. Strangers who ask for money or propose marriage are waving red flags that should not be ignored. But as lonely people seek companionship, online romance scammers will be there to break hearts and empty bank accounts.

Introduction: Losing Billions to Scammers

1. Quoted in Sarah O'Brian, "Tech-Savvy Teens Falling Prey to Online Scams Faster than Their Grandparents," CNBC, August 10, 2021. www.cnbc.com.
2. Kenneth Freundlich, "Why So Many People Fall for Scams," Morris Psychological Group, 2017. https://morrispsych.com.

Chapter One: Phishing, Spear Phishing, and Ransomware

3. Lawrence Abrams, "Tech Support Scammers Lure Victims with Fake Antivirus Billing Emails," BleepingComputer.com, April 8, 2021. www.bleepingcomputer.com.
4. Quoted in Stu Sjouwerman, "Uber Security Breach 'Looks Bad,' Caused by Social Engineering," *KnowBe4* (blog), September 16, 2022. https://blog.knowbe4.com.
5. Quoted in Sara Morrison, "How a Major Oil Pipeline Got Held for Ransom," Vox, June 8, 2021. www.vox.com.
6. Quoted in Terry Gross, "Inner Working of DarkSide Cybergang Reveal It's Run Like Any Other Business," *Fresh Air,* NPR, June 10, 2021. www.npr.org ransomware.
7. Quoted in Bill Heltzel, "Irvington Hacker Ellis Pinsky Agrees to Pay $22 Million in Cryptocurrency Theft," Westchester & Fairfield County Business Journals, November 18, 2022. https://westfaironline.com.
8. Quoted in Ian Sheer, "People Are Fighting Back Against Gift Card Scammers," CNET, November 30, 2021. www.cnet.com.
9. Quoted in Bree Fowler, "Are You Being Scammed? Here's How to Know and What to Do," CNET, December 3, 2021. www.cnet.com.

Chapter Two: Diet and Health Scams

10. Farhad Manjoo, "Alex Jones and the Wellness-Conspiracy Industrial Complex," *New York Times,* August 11, 2022. www.nytimes.com.

11. Quoted in Caitlin Dow, "Problem Pills," *Nutrition Action*, November 2022, p. 10.
12. Quoted in Dani Blum, "Why Is Gut Health Taking Over TikTok?," *New York Times,* April 20, 2022. www.nytimes.com.
13. Quoted in Dan Milmo and Kari Paul, "Facebook Disputes Its Own Research Showing Harmful Effects of Instagram on Teens' Mental Health," *The Guardian,* September 30, 2021. www.theguardian.com.
14. Quoted in Virality Project, *Memes, Magnets, and Microchips: Narrative Dynamics Around COVID-19 Vaccines.* Stanford, CA: Internet Observatory, Stanford University, 2022. https://stacks.stanford.edu/file/druid:mx395xj8490/Virality_project_final_report.pdf.
15. Quoted in Todd Unger, "Pieter Cohen, MD, Explains Dietary Supplements & Regulations," American Medical Association, July 6, 2021. www.ama-assn.org.
16. Malia Frey, "How to Spot a Weight-Loss Scam," Verywell, June 29, 2022. www.verywellfit.com.
17. Quoted in Tiffany Hsu, "As Covid-19 Continues to Spread, So Does Misinformation About It," *New York Times,* December 28, 2022. www.nytimes.com.

Chapter Three: Crypto and Financial Fraud

18. Quoted in Edward Helmore, "Fraud, Cons and Ponzi Schemes: Did Sam Bankman-Fried Use Madoff Tactics?," *The Guardian,* December 17, 2022. www.theguardian.com.
19. Quoted in David Yaffe-Bellany, Matthew Goldstein, and Emily Flitter, "Prosecutors Say FTX Was Engaged in a 'Massive, Yearslong, Fraud," *New York Times,* December 13, 2022. www.nytimes.com.
20. Amanda Hetler, "9 Common Cryptocurrency Scams in 2023," TechTarget, November 2, 2022. www.techtarget.com.
21. Brooke Becher, "What Is a Rug Pull, Exactly?," Built In, November 29, 2022. https://builtin.com.
22. Quoted in Lauren Aratani, "Squid Game Cryptocurrency Collapses in Apparent Scam," *The Guardian,* November 1, 2021. www.theguardian.com.
23. Quoted in David Thomas, "SQUID Ranks as One of the Biggest Crypto Rug Pulls," BeInCrypto, October 26, 2022. https://beincrypto.com.
24. Becher, "What Is a Rug Pull, Exactly?"

25. Quoted in US Securities and Exchange Commission, "SEC Charges Eight Social Media Influencers in $100 Million Stock Manipulation Scheme Promoted on Discord and Twitter," December 14, 2022. www.sec.gov.
26. Quoted in US Attorney's Office, Southern District of Florida, "Three Men Charged in $100 Million Cryptocurrency Fraud," US Department of Justice, June 30, 2022. www.justice.gov.
27. Ben McKenzie, "Is Crypto a Big Scam?," *Deconstructed* (podcast), The Intercept, September 23, 2022. https://theintercept.com.
28. McKenzie, "Is Crypto a Big Scam?"

Chapter Four: Romance Rip-Offs

29. Robin Abcarian, "'Catfishing' Killings Message: Kids are Easy Prey," *Los Angeles Times,* December 7, 2022. www.latimes.com.
30. Quoted in Elly Belle, "Love Bombing: What It Is, and What It Isn't," *Teen Vogue,* February 10, 2022. www.teenvogue.com.
31. Quoted in Alicia Smith, "Police Warn of Romance Scam That Cost Man $80,000," WXYZ Detroit, December 8, 2022. www.wxyz.com.
32. Quoted in Smith, "Police Warn of Romance Scam That Cost Man $80,000."
33. Agari Cyber Intelligence Division, *Scarlet Widow: Breaking Hearts for Profit*. Eden Prairie, MN: Agari, 2022. www.agari.com.
34. Quoted in Agari Cyber Intelligence Division, *Scarlet Widow*.
35. Agari Cyber Intelligence Division, *Scarlet Widow*.
36. Quoted in Adrian Horton, "'Catfishing on a Whole Other Level': The Shocking Story of the Tinder Swindler," *The Guardian,* February 2, 2022. www.theguardian.com.
37. Quoted in Zoe Lake and Lauren Effron, "Woman Says a Man She Met on Tinder Swindled Her Out of $200K: 'He Didn't Just Dump You, He Never Existed,'" ABC News, August 6, 2019. https://abcnews.go.com.
38. Quoted in Horton, "'Catfishing on a Whole Other Level.'"
39. Adryan Corcione, "Catfished Meaning: 14 Signs You're Getting Catfished Online," *Teen Vogue,* September 6, 2022. www.teenvogue.com.
40. Quoted in Corcione, "Catfished Meaning."
41. Kelvin Collins, "Don't Let Romance Scams Break Your Heart," *Augusta (GA) Chronicle*, February 13, 2021. www.augustachronicle.com.

Books

Leah Aguirre and Geraldine O'Sullivan, *The Girl's Guide to Relationships, Sexuality, and Consent*. Oakland, CA: Instant Help, 2022.

Al Desetta, ed., *Healthy Living for Teens: Inspiring Advice on Diet, Exercise, and Handling Stress*. New York: Sky Pony, 2021.

Antoinette King, *The Digital Citizen's Guide to Cybersecurity: How to Be Safe and Empowered Online.* Winter Park, FL: BrightRay, 2022.

Bradley Steffens, *The Dark Side of Social Media*. San Diego: ReferencePoint, 2022.

Jennifer Stephan, *Cyberattacks and Cyberscams: Is There an End in Sight?* San Diego: ReferencePoint, 2023.

Internet Sources

Janet Fowler, "10 Common Scams Targeted at Teens," Investopedia, November 27, 2022. www.investopedia.com.

Amanda Hetler, "9 Common Cryptocurrency Scams in 2023," TechTarget, November 2, 2022. www.techtarget.com.

Adrian Horton, "'Catfishing on a Whole Other Level': The Shocking Story of the Tinder Swindler," *The Guardian*, February 2, 2022. www.theguardian.com.

Farhad Manjoo, "Alex Jones and the Wellness-Conspiracy Industrial Complex," *New York Times,* August 11, 2022. www.nytimes.com.

Ian Sheer, "People Are Fighting Back Against Gift Card Scammers," CNET, November 30, 2021. www.cnet.com.

Websites

Federal Trade Commission (FTC)
www.ftc.gov
The FTC is the official consumer protection agency of the US government. The website offers consumer advice on avoiding

scams involving travel, diet, and employment and directs victims to report identity theft and online fraud.

Fraud.org
www.fraud.org
This is a project of the nonprofit National Consumers League. The site features fraud prevention tips, fraud alerts, informative articles about the latest scams, and links to file complains with authorities in the United States and Canada.

National Institutes of Health (NIH)
https://ods.od.nih.gov/factsheets/list-all
On its webpage titled "Dietary Supplement Fact Sheets," the NIH provides facts about the safety and effectiveness of hundreds of herbs, vitamins, and minerals that are commonly sold by wellness influencers.

News Literacy Project
https://newslit.org
The News Literacy Project teaches young people ways to avoid scams by becoming smart, active consumers of news and information. The site offers an e-learning platform, a free app, podcasts, and shareable tips, tools, and quizzes aimed at increasing media literacy.

Norton
https://us.norton.com
Norton is a leading vender of security software. The "Emerging Threats" link on the Norton site provides comprehensive details about twenty scams, including ransomware, fake shopping sites, and tech support rip-offs.

Note: Boldface page numbers indicate illustrations.

PICTURE CREDITS

Cover: Vasya Kobelev/Shutterstock.com

6: Zamrznuti tonovi/Shutterstock.com
10: Dennizn/Shutterstock.com
13: Hayden Dunsel/Shutterstock.com
18: Eric Broder Van Dyke/Shutterstock.com
22: Vic Hinterlang/Shutterstock.com
25: Universi Digitali/Shutterstock.com
29: Ringo Chiu/Shutterstock.com
34: Everett Collection Inc/Alamy Stock Photo
38: Alamy Stock Photo
41: Oatawa/Shutterstock.com
45: JK/Shutterstock.com
49: NTB/Alamy Stock Photo
53: fiskes/Shutterstock.com

ABOUT THE AUTHOR

Stuart A. Kallen is the author of more than 350 nonfiction books for children and young adults. He has written on topics ranging from the theory of relativity to the art of electronic dance music. In 2018 Kallen won a Green Earth Book Award from the Nature Generation environmental organization for his book *Trashing the Planet: Examining the Global Garbage Glut*. In his spare time, he is a singer, songwriter, and guitarist in San Diego.